21

Ways To Weather the Loss of Your Pet

An Idea Guide To Grieving & Healing

Jean M. Alfieri

All God's Creatures Contributing Author

21 Ways to Weather the Loss of Your Pet

©2025 Jean M. Alfieri

Interior and Cover Design by Christine Sterling-Bortner
Quotes designed by Christine Sterling-Bortner
Images licensed from Adobe Stock (www.stock.adobe.com) and depositphotos.com

IBSN PRINT: 979-8-9896976-4-9

It is better to have loved and lost than never to have loved at all.

~ Alfred Lord Tennyson

Dedication

To all who have loved and lost a beloved pet.

You are not alone. I am sorry for your pain. I hope, like me, you wouldn't trade it for anything in the world.

Grief is intense and unpredictable and does not follow an exact timetable. 21 Ways to Weather the Loss of Your Pet is a valuable resource for someone looking for creative ways to express and manage their feelings about losing their faithful companion. The ideas inside are appropriate for adults and children. As a pet loss therapist, I confidently recommend this book.

21 Ways... is a toolbox that people can pick up and benefit from, at any stage of grief. It can be read from cover to cover or one page at a time. When the person is ready, it can help in processing recent pet loss or loss that happened years ago.

With a heart-centered framework, this book provides practical suggestions and assures readers that there is no wrong way to grieve and no set timeline for healing. It's a comforting companion for those seeking to honor and remember a beloved family pet.

~ Mary Jeanne Murl, LCSW, LMFT
MJ Murl Psychotherapy & Wellness

Table of Contents

Introduction / What's in it for You 6

☙ Before You Begin – Mindset Considerations 10

☙ Part One – Ten Ways to Honor and Remember Your Pet 12

☙ Part Two – Eleven (More Advanced) Project Ideas 33

☙ Part Three – Your Health and Healing 46

From the Author..51

Introduction

It's okay to be sad.

I didn't take it well when my Dad called me at college to tell me our family dog had been put down. I tried desperately to hold the tears at bay until I hung up the phone, but he kept talking. I tried to listen as I wondered how I could go back for the holidays. This animal was really the best part of our home.

Maybe my dad thought so too, as his sadness seeped through the phone line. This man, who only ever spoke in a confident and boisterous voice, agonizingly shared how he held Rumble in his arms. His voice wavered, just slightly.

"Dad, I'm trying not to cry until we end our call. I'm sorry. I'm just so sad."

"It's okay to be sad," he replied. "If we didn't feel sadness, we wouldn't be human. It's okay to be sad."

And with that, I sobbed.

Now, after decades of rescuing senior dogs (my husband and I call them 'vintage puppies'), I offer you the thoughtful activities (beyond crying) that allow me to grieve the loss, embrace the fond memories, and honor the dogs who have been such an integral part of our lives.

"Rescued" is my favorite breed. I have worked as both a volunteer and staff member for the Humane Society of the

Pikes Peak Region, and in short, I'm a dog fanatic. Since we adopt older dogs, we deal with the heartbreak of death more often than most families, but we adore our geriatric canines. (In fact, as I type this, our 18-year-old 'toothless terror' named Reggie sits in my lap. He's a five-pound chihuahua that we adopted when he was 10 years old.)

If you need permission to be sad – here it is.

Your pet will always hold its place in time, and we can't get that time back. So, we grieve the loss. We are sad. And we carry-on, because we must. And we remember those precious moments, when they were funny, protective, cuddly, rambunctious, well-behaved, and not-so-well-behaved.

How can we capture those memories and start healing from the loss? You will find a bounty of ideas here. There are ten basic activities plus eleven more advanced project ideas to honor and remember your beloved pet. Take your time and glance through them. None of them require special talents or skills but some may resonate with you and your situation more than others.

What's in it for You

This book is formatted into four sections:

☙ **Before You Begin** – This section offers a brief consideration of mind-set as you move through this challenging time. Some people consider these activities a distraction, but they are not. These projects provide a way to process your emotions and create a lasting memory for an animal that will forever be a part of your history, and that memory deserves to be honored.

☙ **Part One** – This section presents ten ways to grieve the loss of your pet through writing and art projects. It outlines a variety of activities to create mementos and tributes, using words, drawings, pictures. The ideas are simple and straightforward and can accommodate all skills levels. They appeal to all ages. Try one or try them all.

Throughout this section, you also receive ten single words to help you weather the loss and encourage you on your journey of healing.

☙ **Part Two** – This section gives you eleven more advanced ideas that will require a bit more patience and time. There are ideas for every budget, and some also make nice memorial gifts for others.

☙ **Part Three** – This section provides some coping considerations for your overall health. It may be a challenge to think about your physical, mental, or emotional well-being when grief weighs heavy on your heart. But your overall health is a key factor to moving forward on the path to healing.

This book delivers a full 'survival toolkit' of ways to grieve the passing of your pet by capturing the happy memories of their life. Let your imagination soar as these ideas prompt even more ideas. By the time you finish reading this book your survival toolkit will be brimming as well.

Before You Begin
Mindset Considerations

When an animal family member dies, everyone feels the loss. Each person will process their sadness differently. Even if this is not the first time you've experienced the death of pet, it may impact you in a way you don't expect. Why? This pet is different than the other. You are in a different place in life than you were before. Maybe there are more or fewer people who are impacted by the loss.

Three Main Points:

1. You have permission to be sad.

Don't let anyone try to minimize your pain. Some people won't understand but you don't have to apologize for feeling the heartache. You are experiencing a significant loss. This was an animal that will forever be a part of your history. Your memory of them deserves to be honored.

Consider the grief you are feeling. It is impossible to help other family members cope with this loss if you haven't first faced your own sadness.

2. Allow yourself some grace.

There is no set period to mourn. Don't expect that one day, one week, or one month is sufficient time to grieve. There is not a set timeframe in which your heart will automatically heal. There may be gaps in the family dynamic that you didn't realize until a special occasion or anniversary comes along.

3. *Be patient with yourself – and each other.*

Recognize how others can support you. Sometimes it helps to have someone to sit with you in your suffering. And sometimes you are called to be the person that sits with another who is brokenhearted.

Losing a pet is difficult at any age. It can be exceptionally hard for seniors, especially if the pet was the last living member in their household. Having already dealt with a lifetime of loss this trauma can feel worse than normal grief. If you know a senior who has lost a pet, check in with them. Offer to talk or assist them in creating a lasting memory of their special family member.

If you have children, younger ones may spend less time mourning while older kids might struggle more than they let on. Consider if they had an after-school or bed-time routine with the pet and how the pet's absence now leaves a gap in their day.

At any age, annual events like birthdays and holidays may trigger unexpected surges of sadness and linger longer than expected.

Part One

Ten Ways to Honor and Remember Your Pet

1. Create a "memorial" rock.

Find a large flat rock, a pavestone, or a broken piece of cinderblock. Paint the pet's name, surrounded by flowers, pawprints, or a rainbow. Find a special place to display.

Note: If you are painting inside, protect the table (or painting area) with sheets of newspaper (or other covering) before you start. This will minimize clean-up of any paint splatter or spills.

Also, acrylic paint works best.

Gratitude

It may be hard to have a heart of gratitude when your sorrow runs so deep. As you grieve, don't let all the happiness they brought get buried. Be sure to focus on the good times you shared with this pet. Whether your time together was long or short, there is much to be thankful for.

2. Write a note to the pet.

Say good-bye in your own words. You can write a letter directly to your pet.

Help kids capture their feelings and remember this is an emotionally challenging time. Respect their privacy if they don't want assistance or to share their letter.

You can leave the note(s) in a specially designated place or on the pet's favorite bed or resting spot.

Here's a page to help you get started. You can color in the border or add other embellishments. Cut along the dotted line to remove.

Honor

Showing one's respect, whether toward a person or a pet, is a great honor. A pet who has been with you through the difficulties of life deserves to be remembered. There are so many ways to do that and however you choose to honor your pet is perfect.

3. Tell your favorite stories.

Gather the family and let everyone share their favorite memory of your pet. It's sure to bring smiles. You may even be surprised at the many different stories and happy times that beautiful spirit inspired.

Smile

Your pet would want you to be happy, right? It's okay to smile – even laugh at the memory of a funny antic or occasion. That's how you come to terms with their passing; by appreciating the life and love they shared with you. What a beautiful legacy to leave with you.

~ Bonus Idea ~

Create a "Memory Bowl" - Write down assorted brief happy memories of your pet on colorful pieces of paper and drop them into a bowl. Younger children can draw pictures. When feeling a surge of sadness over the loss, grab a happy memory to lift your spirits.

Here is some space to capture those funny antics and special times that made you laugh. Cut out and drop in your memory bowl.

Happy Memories!

4. Read a book about pet loss.

Go to your favorite on-line book-site and search: *books about losing a pet*. Or call your local bookstore. Some books tell a story while others are interactive so don't rush your selection. Take time to scroll through the wide variety of options.

Love

The love that created your precious bond doesn't fade in their absence. Though your heart is broken, your memories can grow fonder. Hold them close and allow them to help your heart heal. Awaken to all the love that surrounds you.

5. Draw and/or color a picture of your pet.

Like writing, art can be a creative and therapeutic outlet. A freehand drawing is another unique way to honor your pet's life.

Not super artistic? Here's a tip to outline the picture:

- 🐾 Lightly tape a favorite photo on the backside of a piece of paper so you can see the image through the paper.

- 🐾 Trace the photo with a pencil. Outline as many details as possible.

- 🐾 Gently remove the photo and shade or color the picture.

Freehand drawing or outlining a picture makes the connection to that memory even more personal. When you're done you can frame and display it in a special place.

Remember

What a wonderful legacy your pet has left with you. Not just in memories of their snuggles and playfulness, but in pictures of special moments and occasions. Remembering their loyal companionship is a tribute to the love and life they dedicated to you.

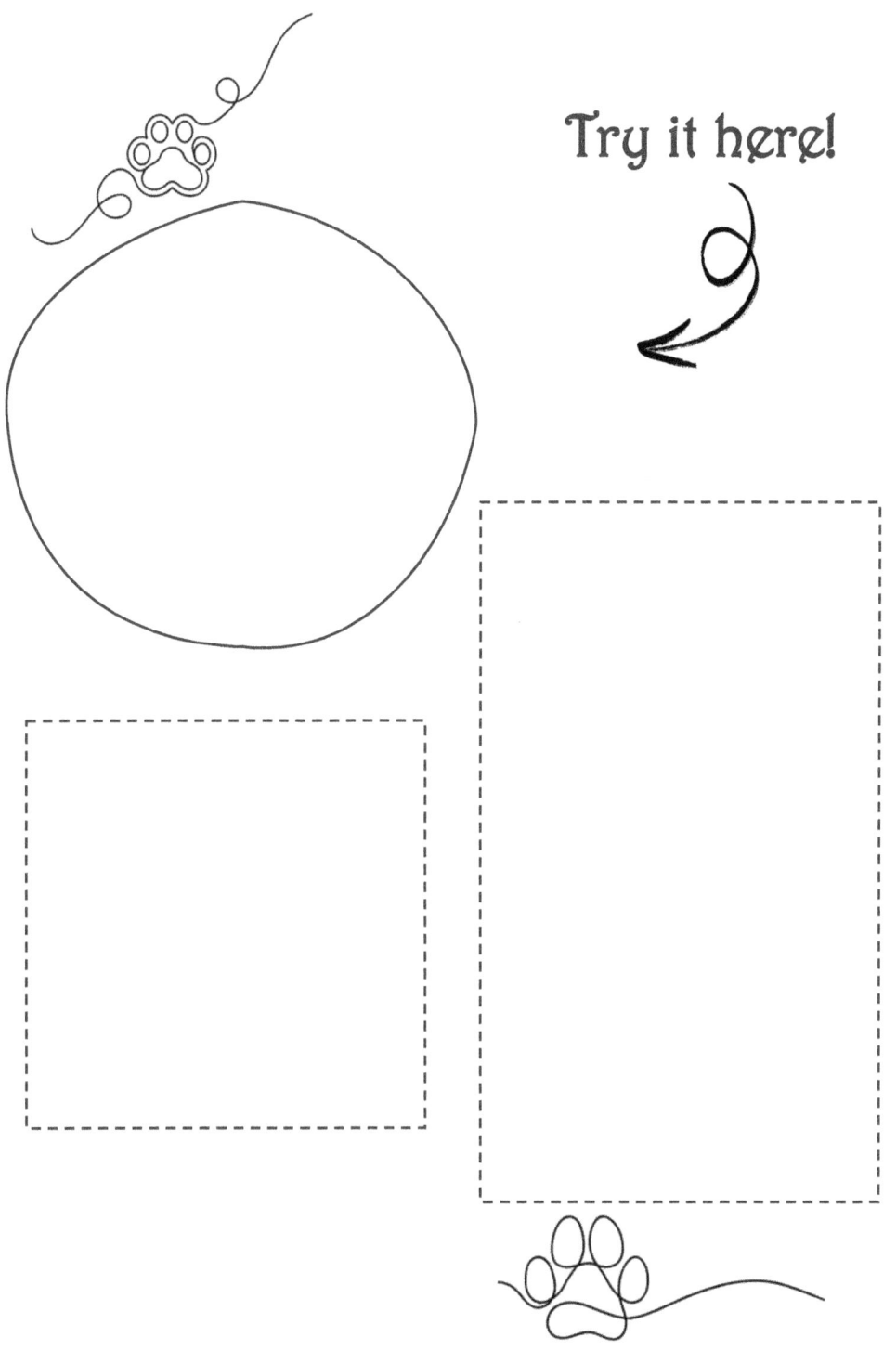

Try it here!

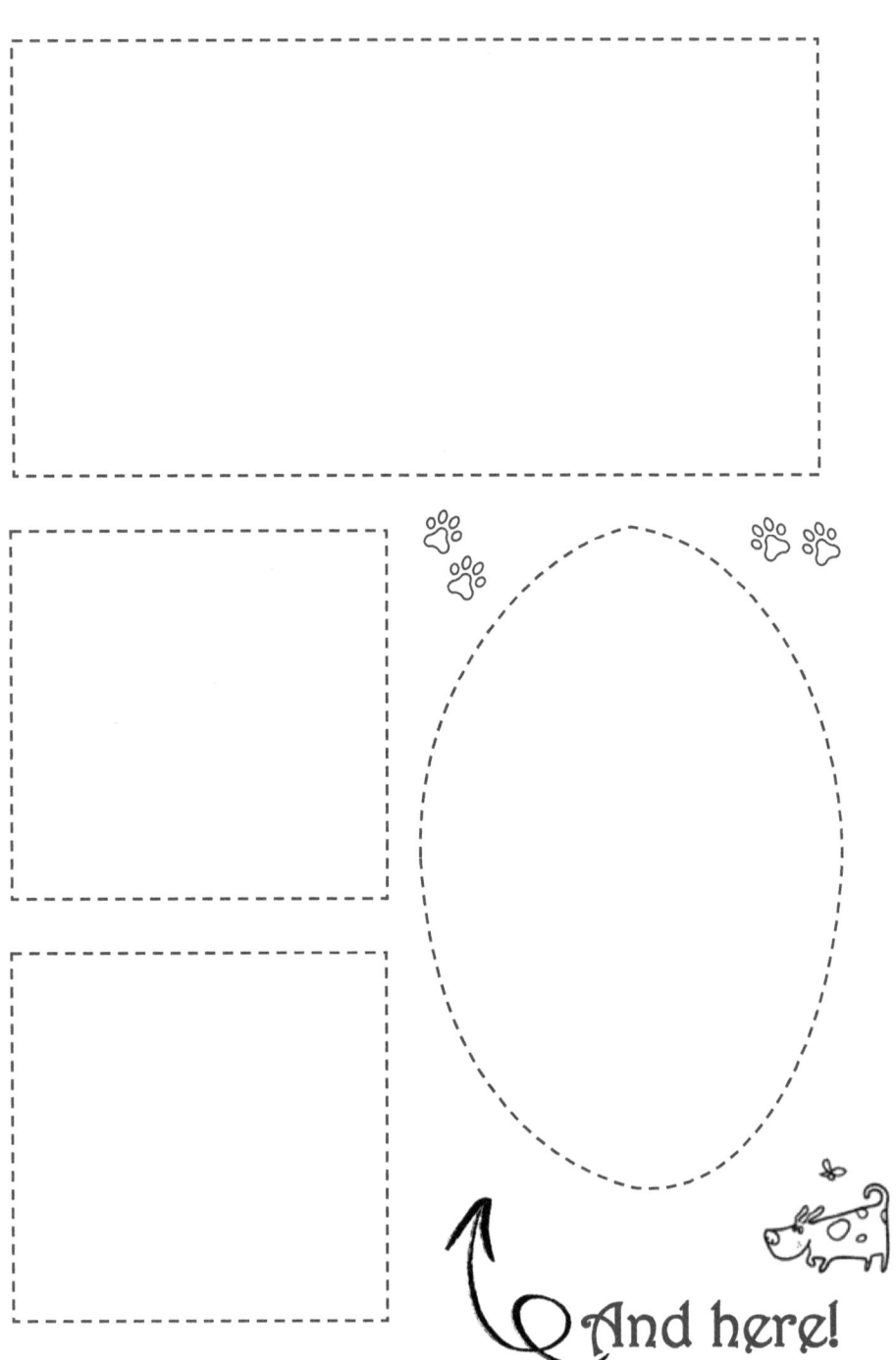

And here!

6. Design a collage.

This is a great visual collection of memories. It can be done online. I recommend taking the time to manually assemble the collage, especially if doing this project with kids.

- 🐾 Sort through your digital collection and print pictures from all stages of your pet's life.

- 🐾 Crop the pictures as desired and arrange.

- 🐾 Use a pre-designed frame or special backing paper to ensure longevity.

- 🐾 Be sure to use acid-free photo glue so the pictures aren't damaged.

Embrace

Hold your whole assortment of memories close. There was so much about your pet to love. Give thanks for the time, the love, and the laughter you enjoyed. Your pet was no doubt one of a kind. What a special blessing in your life.

~ Bonus Idea ~

Go a step further and …

🐾 Add ribbon, fabric or other natural materials to add texture.

🐾 Hand-write single words and glue next to the photos to describe how that event made you feel.

🐾 Include captions or short notes to document the dates and details of the events.

7. Make a mini scrapbook – or a full-size book!

You can find many page-design ideas online. This can be as big or small a project as you want. It doesn't have to follow a certain order or capture every detail.

- ❧ Include pictures with short captions. Include the date, place, and event.

- ❧ Allow space for longer notes. Jot down the best part of the day or what you love about the pictures. (Describe your feelings.)

- ❧ Find (or make) special embellishments. Decorate the page with strips of colorful paper, buttons, ribbon, stickers, etc.

Reflect

The loss is more than a discomforting shift in your routine. There was something special about your time together and what that animal's spirit brought to you.

- ❧ How was this pet a reflection of your life?
- ❧ What made that pet, during its time with you, such a remarkable fit?
- ❧ What made you so compatible?

8. Create an ornament - featuring your pet's picture.

You may have some endearing memories of your pet during the holidays. Ornaments are a unique way to treasure them. You can also enjoy them throughout the year. Hang them in a window, on a flowerpot or vase, or set them on a shelf for a special keepsake.

Research DIY decorations.

🐾 You can buy ornament frames of varied sizes.

🐾 There are also online stores that will create one from your uploaded photo.

🐾 You can make your own.

One of my favorites is the box ornament because it displays six pictures – one on each side, top, and bottom, so you can enjoy a different image simply by turning it.

Thankful

Take a moment to look at this wonderful relationship from your pet's point of view. Your pet was well cared for and loved because of you. Consider how thankful they were for YOU being their person. And now you have a collection of joyous memories to carry forward.

Create an Ornament.

Design a jewelry memento.

9. Design a jewelry memento.

🐾 Make a bracelet with colorful beads and letters that spell out your pet's name.

🐾 Customize a locket necklace with a tiny picture of you and your pet

🐾 Create a custom keychain with a special picture or the pet's name

~ Bonus Idea ~

Is there someone else who misses this pet? Make a unique memento for yourself and another to give as a gift.

Walk

There are many walks in life. Some are physical, others are spiritual. Some walks include other people. Some include our pets. They are all part of our journey and the walks we take with pets are extra grand.

10. Decorate a T-shirt.

🐾 Use fabric paint or a permanent marker to draw pictures, doodles, and words that represent your pet. Make it big and elaborate, small and sweet, or a combination of both.

🐾 Keep it simple with black ink/paint on a white t-shirt or use assorted paint color or markers for a more vibrant design.

🐾 Consider adding words like friendly, loyal, happy, sassy, playful, etc. Remember to include your pet's name.

Pause

Take a moment for yourself. Pause to reflect. To remember. To appreciate the gift of your pet. These activities are designed to help. Still, they can't completely fill the gap. Be patient with the healing process and your progress along the way.

Check it out!

Part Two

Eleven (More Advanced) Project Ideas

Explore some of these more advanced ideas and let your creativity flow. The healing process is not about skill level or even the final piece. The focus is the tribute to your lost pet.

1. Paint a tile or a wine glass.

Do some online research for directions on your specific project.

(Example: glassware requires special paint and needs to be 'finished' by heating the painted glass in the oven. It must also be hand-washed.)

Painted tiles (with a paw print or heart encircling the pet's name) make great memorials and gifts for others who had a special bond with the pet.

2. Compose a eulogy.

The word 'Eulogy' means to offer high praise; to bless, or speak well of. We do it for people, we can do it for pets by listing their defining qualities and amazing attributes.

Consider a brief (two or three sentence) description for each person (and other fur family members) that your animal touched and describe their connection. You can keep a longer version for yourself and share a shorter version on social media. It's a thoughtful way to deliver the news without having to reach out to individuals and retell the sad details.

When we lost our 12-year-old Airedale to cancer, my husband and I wrote a eulogy and shared it on Facebook. It felt good to recall the love and joy she brought to our whole family (other dogs, included) and our friends appreciated knowing she had passed.

Eulogy Framework:

Here are the elements to include when composing a eulogy.

Introduction:

- 🐾 Pet's Name / nickname(s)

- 🐾 When and how you adopted

- 🐾 How long they were with you

Body:

- 🐾 The special way the pet interacted with each person in your family or circle of friends

- 🐾 How the pet interacted with other family pets

Closing:

- 🐾 One or two short sentences on how/why the pet passed away (illness, age, etc.)

- 🐾 A special trait or quirky attribute by which you will always remember this pet

- 🐾 Final reflection / express gratitude for the privilege of honoring them

This is the eulogy I posted after the death of our beautiful Silly Sally:

After submitting our application to the Airedale Rescue, we waited a year for Sal. It wasn't that there were no Airedales in need of adoption, but they are hunting dogs, and by nature, have a high prey drive. It is few and far between that you can find one willing to tolerate small family dogs or cats.

Sally didn't just tolerate our pack of little loafs, she was a champion big sister. Her head was as big as Reggie's entire body.

Yet, when he barked at her, she would feign being frightened and run the other way, encouraging him to chase her. The two of them were hilarious.

Regularly, while Sally tried to nap on her bed, Zoey would blindly walk into or across her head. Sally would simply lift her nose and redirect the lost pug. Often, Zoey would decide to stay right there and lay down next to Sally.

And whenever Morty stood at the screen door and barked at absolutely nothing, Sally would run over and provide several big-dog barks to back him up.

She was even more than a rock-star fur-sister. She was a faithful walking partner to me. The little dogs easily tire out and turn around after a half-block, but Sally loved hitting the trails. She made sure I noticed all the highlights, whether it was deer, squirrels, or a pretty flower.

And Sally was the best greeter when Josh returned from work. As soon as the garage door opened, she'd eagerly wait for his entrance. I tried to be as enthusiastic but couldn't compete with the dancing and prancing every evening as he entered the house. It was truly a celebration whenever Dad came home.

Sally's health declined over the past month, complications from the cancerous tumors on her leg and stomach. It became clear that it was time to say farewell. I'm grateful to the compassionate Vet team that went so far as to prepare Sally a Thanksgiving plate of sliced ham, mac & cheese and sweet potatoes. She loved it all and rested her head peacefully on Josh's knee as she went to sleep.

Sally will forever hold her place in our hearts and I'm beyond thankful to have had this sweet and silly pup in our lives.

3. Journal your favorite stories.

Try some of these prompts about your precious pet. You can capture the stories here and cut this page out to frame. Or, write them in your personal journal, in a memory book, or on a paper you can display as a keepsake.

- 🐾 I remember when we met. It was _____ (time of year) at _____ (location).

- 🐾 How you got your name.

- 🐾 You had some great nicknames.

- 🐾 Your favorite / least favorite outfit.

- 🐾 The goofy thing you always did.

- 🐾 Your favorite treat / favorite people-snack.

- 🐾 I couldn't stop laughing when you …

- 🐾 When people came over, you would …

- 🐾 You loved it when …

- 🐾 Our greatest adventure.

- 🐾 Your favorite place to nap.

- 🐾 The best toy ever.

4. Create a video tribute.

🐾 Store it on a thumb drive or share on social media.

🐾 Have each family member offer ideas of their favorite pictures and video clips.

🐾 Let the most tech-savvy family member or friend compile them into a video set to a favorite song.

5. Plan a 'Memorial' Event.

If you received your pet's ashes, plan an outing (or road trip) to one of your pet's favorite places and sprinkle them along the trail or shoreline or favorite tree.

🐾 Keep some of the ashes – and display them in a special place *(see shadowbox)*.

🐾 No ashes – no problem. Go on a 'memorial' walk or hike down your pet's favorite street or most often covered trail. Pause where they would pause and tell them how you feel.

6. Assemble a Shadowbox.

Collect small mementos (their collar, name tag, clay pawprint, favorite toy, etc.), add some pictures, short stories or clips of happy memories and assemble in a shadow box. Research other content ideas online.

7. Write your pet's story.

How did you meet or find your pet? (Or did your pet find you?) Where did your relationship begin?

This can be written from your point of view OR write about the experience from your pet's perspective.

~ Bonus Idea ~

Read it aloud to someone or record a video of your reading and share it on social media.

8. Create a vision board about your pet's "superpower."

Were they a super-napper, super-snacker, or a super-supporter of yours? Pets bring so much joy to our lives. They can console us when we're sad and cheer for us when we're happy.

- 🐾 Make a list of 10 – 15 words that best describe your pet's superpower.

- 🐾 Search for pictures and images that match those words.

- 🐾 Compile and arrange the collection of pictures in a document. (Canva and PowerPoint can be great tools for this project)

- 🐾 Crop the images to fit whatever size and orientation (portrait or landscape) you prefer, depending on where you want to display the vision board. (Use as a screen saver, cell phone wallpaper, or print to display in a special place.)

Scout

12.7.2024

9. Create a list
(like a last will and testament).

If your pet were to create a list of all the things they would have left for you, what would it include?

This won't look like a (human) list of physical objects, though it may include some special pet items that you have.

It may be that they leave you peace and joy, just like you felt upon returning home to them. Or the calm feeling you would get whenever they brushed up against you.

10. Host your own paint-n-sip (or do it solo).

🐾 Get a blank canvas and some paints and see what happens. Paint an abstract picture of your pet or print their name and decorate the letters with flowers and vines.

🐾 Gather the family or a group of friends and pull up pictures you'd each like to paint. It can be a different image for everyone. (Perhaps they have a pet they'd like to paint.) Easy to follow directions for this can be found online.

Remember, abstracts are unique to each person so there's no worry about being perfect. Each one will be special in its own way.

~ Bonus Idea (for kids) ~

If you have little ones, consider a finger-painting party.

Be sure to save their tribute in a special place.

11. Take a ceramics class.

Select a piece of dishware that you can customize. Plates and coffee mugs make great canvases. Paint a paw print with the pet's name or (more advanced) paint the pet's face.

Easier option: Photo sites (like Walgreens and Shutterfly) offer different ways in which to add favorite photos to a variety of items, including travel mugs. Check out the many different options.

Can't choose one photo? Assemble a mini collage of pictures. Track your pet's life from young to old or choose a theme, like a family vacation.

~ Bonus Idea ~

12. Hold the space for routines that used to involve your pet.

We tend to miss our pet most during the parts of the day that we used to spend time with them. Whether you fed them at a certain hour or took them for a daily walk, you can hold that space by lighting a candle. (Consider using battery operated candles for safety.)

This helps us to acknowledge their absence and marks our sorrow so that time of day doesn't seem so empty.

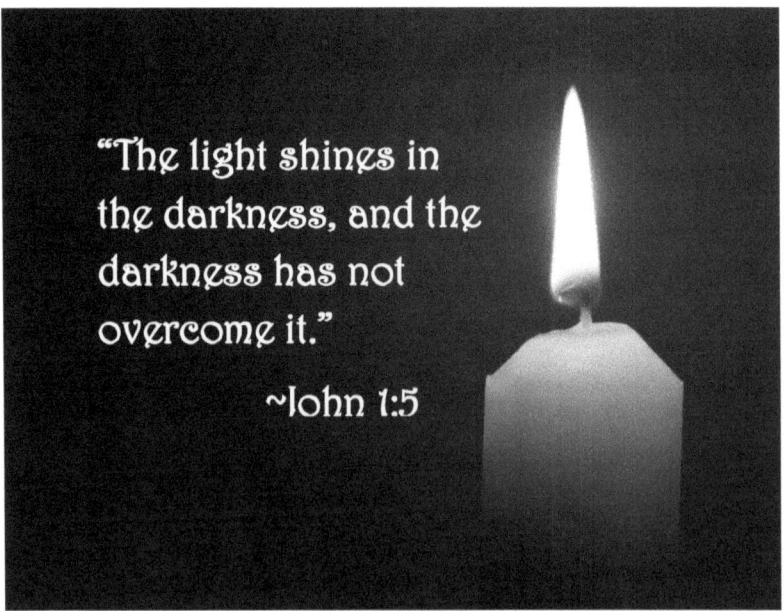

"The light shines in the darkness, and the darkness has not overcome it."

~John 1:5

Part Three

YOUR HEALTH AND HEALING

Take note of your overall health. You have a special bond with your animal family members. When one passes on, it can be devastating. The loss can take an emotional, physical, even spiritual toll.

~ The Five Stages of Grief: ~

- 🐾 **Denial or disbelief** – you don't want to admit or acknowledge the loss.

- 🐾 **Anger or resentment** – you feel agitated or resentful toward yourself, others, or the pet, for creating this situation.

- 🐾 **Bargaining** – you pray to make a deal with God to change the situation.

- 🐾 **Depression or discouragement** – you sink into feelings of emptiness and despair.

- 🐾 **Acceptance and release** – you come to terms with the loss and can move forward. The sadness may resurface but you are able to find joy in life.

The process of grieving is not linear. It is a winding river. Consider where you are within it. The length of time you sit in any stage is unique to you. Your grief journey may follow the winding river. It is common that once you move through one stage you might circle back and revisit it at some point.

There will be situations and events that bring back a flood of memories, and with that, the pain of loss. Take heart – you are still making progress.

Remember to take care of yourself during this time.

~ Tips for Coping: ~

1. Try to stay on track. It will take time to heal. Allow yourself to grieve but don't abandon your normal routine. It may be difficult when you don't feel like getting out of bed or eating but taking care of your physical health is important. Take little steps every day to stay on track with your exercise, work, and meal routines.

2. Surround yourself with people who get it. Other pet-parents understand the pain of your loss. They can allow you to talk through your feelings, offering sympathy and support and may offer coping techniques that they have discovered. But remember, each situation is unique and do what you need to cope.

3. Explore healthy ways to process your loss. Talking is good therapy. Painting, creating a memorial, and other artistic outlets can be therapeutic. Try journaling about your beloved pet. Capturing the memories will allow you to appreciate and enjoy the special life and bond you shared.

4. Know when to seek professional help. Sitting for a while in sadness is different than the misery of despair.

Depression is a serious health condition. Find a support group and /or see your doctor if you become depressed. Grief can take a serious toll. Get the help you need so you can move forward and care for yourself and those around you.

I loved you your whole life.

I'll miss you for the rest of mine.

From the Author

I remember when the inkling for this book first began:

I sat in a big wooden rocking chair in the middle of the 2nd grade class. They sat in a semi-circle on the floor surrounding me. This class had won a personal visit with "the author," and were prepared to pepper me with questions. I hoped to live up to their expectations.

They lobbed some soft pitches:

"When will you write a chapter book?"

"How old were you when you started writing stories?"

"What's your favorite breed of dog?"

Then came the knuckle ball:

"Have you ever had a dog that died?"

Such a painful, raw, and honest question from a seven-year-old.

"Yes, I have," I said, "We've had dogs a long time. But it always makes me sad. We have a tradition that when one of our dogs dies, we celebrate their memory at dinner that night. We share our favorite stories of them and always end up laughing and crying," I paused then added, "Did your dog die?"

Ben nodded and stared down into his hands.

"Do you have a favorite memory of your dog?"

He looked up, eyes watery, and said, "He always waited for me to come home from school."

My heart broke for him. "I know, Ben, that's so hard. What was your dog's name?"

"Benji."

"I'm sorry that Benji died. It's okay to miss him. I still miss my first dog named Rumble. He died when I was in college way back in 1988!"

The class gave a collective gasp as if to say, "You were alive in 1988?!"

"I know," I admitted, feeling ancient. "Has anyone else had a dog that died?"

A spattering of hands went up.

"Maybe during lunch or over a break you can share your favorite story of your dog with Ben, and that might cheer him up."

Their heads nodded.

"And remember, Ben, even though he may not be waiting for you after school, Benji will always be in your heart."

I had no idea I had visited that day to start a 2nd grade therapy group, but the reality is, it doesn't matter your age. Losing a beloved companion is devastating.

Since you have this book, you are likely experiencing the loss of a beloved animal family member. My heart is heavy for your loss. I hope these projects and ideas bring some relief and help you and your family embrace the fond memories of your pet. I wish you peace and love as you heal.

Condolences,

Jean

"If there ever comes a day where we can't be together, keep me in your heart. I'll stay there forever. – A. A. Milne, Winnie the Pooh

About the Author

Jean Alfieri is an author, speaker, and dog fan. She worked for over 30 years in human resources and professional development in public and private industries. As an undertaking of this book project, she became a certified grief coach for pet loss. She now splits her time between writing and consulting.

When her eyes locked with those of a smooshy-faced little dog who sat inside a kennel at the local animal shelter, it was love! He captured her heart, and she captures their many adventures in short stories starring *Zuggy the Rescue Pug*.

Jean and her husband joke that although they pay the mortgage of their home in Colorado, it's really the dogs' house. She finds much of her writing inspiration from her senior pups and work at the Pikes Peak Humane Society. Find out more @DogAuthor.com.

DON'T FORGET
SOMEWHERE
BETWEEN 🐾
THE *Hello*
🐾
🐾 AND THE
Good-bye
THERE WAS 🐾
🐾 🐾 *Love*
so much
LOVE

www.ingramcontent.com/pod-product-compliance
Lightning Source LLC
Chambersburg PA
CBHW051648120626
46551CB00015B/2263

* 9 7 9 8 9 8 9 6 9 7 6 4 9 *